# Relationships:
## Overcoming Ungodly Soul Ties & Emotional Injuries

# Study Guide

## DR. MARY M. GEORGE

# Relationships: Overcoming Ungodly Soul Ties & Emotional Injuries

## Study Guide

*Copyright © 2013*
*Dr. Mary M. George*

*ISBN: 0-9785185-2-7*

*CONTACT INFORMATION:*

**Balm in Gilead Ministries (Big Ministries)**
*Website: www.bigministries.net*
**Dr. Mary M. George**
*dr.maryg@bigministries.net*

# *Dedication*

*In dedication to the memory of my loving sister*

*Hattie L. Miller*

*who was a great inspiration and support to me.*

*May your prayers continue in my behalf, and forever will my love stretch*

*toward your memory.*

This study guide book is part of the workshop *"Relationships: Overcoming Ungodly Soul ties and Emotional Injuries"* –that is facilitated by Dr. Mary M. George.

It is designed to bring transparency and balance to relationships many have entered into impulsively by:

- not asking the right questions,
- providing too much information about oneself,
- ignoring red flags,
- being too permissive,
- compromising morals, values, and faith, or
- confounding true love with false love.

Dr. George keeps it real with her participants as she guides them through The BAR: *being attentive and responsive in your relationship and its course.*

The relationships many have entered into impulsively have turned out to be unhealthy or imbalanced. This is due to becoming negligent in the relationship, not setting boundaries, and not being attentive to the many courses a relationship can take. This carelessness has allowed the relationship to move off –course into unhealthiness, causing someone to become injured.

Participants in the workshop can expect to receive understanding in the importance of The BAR, and healing for those who have acquired emotional scars from unhealthy relationships.

*Relationships study guide is divided into four segments:*

Chapter 1:    Keeping It Real!

Chapter 2:    THE BAR: Be Attentive and Responsive in the –Relationship and its Course

Chapter 3:    Sexuality of "Man"

Chapter 4:    Emotional Healing

# *Chapter 1*

Hello,

We are part of Dr. George's prayer team. We will be sharing powerful points at the begining of each chapter to reinforce and mobilize you into ACTION!

CHAPTER 1

# Keeping It Real!

---

Incomplete vs. Un-fulfilled

Defining Various Forms of Dating

Protect / Crucify

The Price I'm Willing to Pay?

## Incomplete vs. Unfulfilled

Man and woman were originally created coequal, until the fall in the garden *(Genesis 1:27-28; 3:15-17)*; at that point God placed order in the family. This order consists of the husband as the head of his family, and his wife to assist him in fulfilling the purpose and ministry of that marriage and family.

Both men and women need to feel loved and be in relationship with God. God created man to be respected, and honored in his home. God's intent for man is to accept and respond honorably to his responsibilities as the leader in his home. God created woman to be submitted to her husband, honor, respect, and support him. God created her to be multi-gifted in her role as "help" to her husband. A woman must feel appreciated and protected by her husband. She must feel external affections and security –this is not just sex, but she wants to be held, talked to, taken out on dates, financially supported, be a partner, part of a team with her husband.

Single church women are viewed by some in our society today as being wild, naïve, lonely and anxious to be married. We must put an end to this repulsive stereotyping of single church women. There are single church women who are:

- well educated,
- responsible,
- hardworking,
- multitalented,
- homeowners,
- building owners and managers,
- CEO of corporations,
- owners of fabulous automobiles, and
- knowledgeable about the stock market!

They are active in sports and make great mothers and homemakers. We have to be careful as kingdom women of what we are projecting to this world. We represent the kingdom of God and must carry ourselves as kingdom people living according to God's principles.

I have known single church women to say they feel incomplete without a man, but I beg to differ with them; after God created mankind, he said, "IT IS VERY GOOD!"

I say to every single woman who shares this feeling of being incomplete without a man, this is not true: you may feel unfulfilled in that particular area in your life, but you are not incomplete. I believe many times, singles lose focus of their immediate *(current)* purpose. Paul brings clarity to singles' immediate role: "*....leading to so many more demands on your attention. The time and energy that married people spend on caring for and nurturing*

*each other, the unmarried can spend in becoming whole and holy instruments of God."*
*1 Corinthians 7:34(MSG)*

This is not to be looked upon as just reading the Bible, praying and going to church. You are to be in relationship with God obtaining your purpose and calling, receiving daily directions and instructions. If he is calling you to pastor, enroll in a seminary or a Christian college, or complete one or two units of CPE –clinical pastoral education -give God something to work with by participating in your preparation; direct your mind and energy toward preparing for what God is calling you into.

**Reflections:**

# Defining Various Forms of Dating

There are social pressures today that lean increasingly toward provocative sexual relations and behavior. Today's congregants –church people –are being enticed more and more by society's various forms of dating and depraved acts of sexual gratification. The involvement of God's people in these immoral activities grieves the Holy Spirit:

**New King James Version (NKJV)**
And do not grieve the Holy Spirit of God, by whom you were sealed for the day of redemption.
Ephesians 4:30

**The Message (MSG)**
Don't grieve God. Don't break his heart. His Holy Spirit, moving and breathing in you, is the most intimate part of your life, making you fit for him. Don't take such a gift for granted.

- **CHRISTIAN DATING -** involves dating behaviors that are based upon the person's religious beliefs.

- **ONLINE DATING -** is where people meet and get to know each other over the Internet instead of in person. People often connect through chat, and email, and exchange photos online. Once a connection is made, they often arrange an in-person meeting.

- **SPEED DATING -** is generally set up by an organization or dating service. People arrive at a designated location and quickly spend one-on-one time with other dating candidates. The time spent with each dating candidate varies from five to ten minutes. Speed dating allows people to meet several dating candidates in one setting to see if any are suitable matches.

- **DOUBLE DATING -** is where couples go out together. Double dating is popular among teenagers, adult couples who have similar interests and people on blind dates.

- **A FRIEND WITH BENEFITS -** is a friend with whom one has sex with no strings attached. There is no committed relationship.

- **BLIND DATING -** is where two people who do not know each other are set up by someone else to go on a date. Blind dates are usually arranged by friends, family, or co-workers.

- **CASUAL DATING –** IS when a person dates many people. Casual dating is done by people: who are not interested in settling down with one person, who are searching for the right partner to settle down with, or who are just looking for sexual relationships.

- **SERIOUS DATING –** IS when two people date only each other, and they consider themselves a couple. Serious dating involves a commitment and monogamy (committed-stable). This type of dating often leads to becoming engaged and married.

**Reflections:**

## Protect / Crucify

The enemy has deceived God's people by directing their focus to be totally attentive to **not fornicating.** I'm not saying fornication is alright; the Bible says "...fornicators shall not inherit the kingdom of God...." Galatians 5:19-21.

What I am saying is sometimes we can become so focused on one thing we lose sight of another that is equally important. Allowing Satan this move of manipulation can cause you to become deceived by his strategies. You will hear me say over and over again: **Satan's play book never changes –only his players**. He is not creative; he copies everything God does and uses it for evil.

Making the act of not fornicating your sol priority leaves a crucial area in your life vulnerable to a major attack by the enemy. What is this crucial area: it's your mind! You must protect it as you crucify your flesh!

This is what the enemy really wants; once he can apprehend this area he is in control to manipulate whatever action he desires from you.

Often Christians enter into relationships and become so focused on disciplining the flesh, and not yielding to fornication they forget they have left a vital door unattended for the enemy to enter and do great damage!

This unattended door is the entrance to your thought process, for the purpose of manipulation. Allowing access through this door can cause you to become influenced in ways that are un-favorable to you. This can easily lead to an unhealthy relationship where you can become misused and abused.

You have accomplished constraining your flesh; but now you can find yourself in a battle within your mind! These battles encompass your emotions, desires, guilt for not pleasing others, and the compromising of your morals and values to make others happy.

There was a time when your thoughts and feelings were all about God, but now they are centered elsewhere: pleasing and attending to the needs of the flesh (not just yours). You began the process of compromising your Christian beliefs through thoughts in your mind. Your communication line to God become interrupted with static, which now you from hearing God. The reason being, Satan had you focus on the front door while he was slipping through the back door.

*Illustration*: I will use lust as an example. Satan manipulates you to achieve his goals through what you *hear, see, feel,* and *think*. He stimulates these areas for a door to be opened to the spirit of lust.

Sin escalates, so once lust enters it takes you deeper into sin. You may start with masturbation and Satan convinces you it's okay; you are not having sex with anyone and no one is being hurt. The next steps he can lead you to are sex toys, fornication, and pornography and they will keep taking you farther and farther from God. What Satan did not want you to know is that once you give him entrance, you have given him permission to come in and have access to your body to stimulate and manipulate his desires.

**New King James Version** (NKJV)

But I say to you that whoever looks at a woman to lust for her has already committed adultery with her in his heart.

Matthew 5:28

**The Message** (MSG)

But don't think you've preserved your virtue simply by staying out of bed. Your heart can be corrupted by lust even quicker than your body. Those leering looks you think nobody notices - they also corrupt.

It is very important not to compromise your faith as you protect your mind and body from being manipulated and controlled by another in the relationship. This can easily happen when you compromise your *morals, and values* in order to please the other person in the relationship.

This course of action leads to unhealthiness, because one person in the relationship is now gaining power and control over the other. That person will manipulate the other's emotions and actions with the absolute intent of securing personal gratification for him or herself, even though these tactics will cause emotional injuries for the other person.

The injured individual's only recourse is to get back to God as quickly as possible with the determination of Jacob –**"I'm not going to let you go until you bless me!"** –and that blessing is inner healing, wisdom, and the understanding of true love.

Before you become involved in an interpersonal relationship, ask questions about the individual: employment, education, the family that raised him/her, and previous relationships. If he/she hasn't stayed in one place long, ask why –you deserve to know. This person is about to enter your world and join your inner circle, touching the lives of your loved ones. Not inquiring can inflame much drama that will leave you emotionally and physically wounded traumatized and/or terrorized!

Meet the person's family! What are mom and dad like, and how do they relate? How does the family interact, together and with others? What do the sisters, brothers, nieces, and nephews have going on for them? What's up with Aunt Lula and Uncle Bob fighting every weekend?

**COMMUNICATE, OBSERVE AND ACKNOWLEDGE WHAT YOU HAVE OBSERVED.**
This gives you the information you need to assess whether to continue the relationship or not. The relationship assessment should include, but not be limited to their:

→ Faith and culture,

→ Relations with family and others,

→ goals in life,

→ employment, and

→ problem solving and anger management.

Once this assessment is complete you and God can decide if this is the will of God for your life. Your summation will reveal what this relationship will cost you *(spiritually, emotionally, mentally, and physically),* and you will have to ask yourself if this relationship is worth the price you will pay to maintain it.

You can count on this: if Uncle Bob and Dad are beating on their wives you can expect to have some encounters with violence in your relationship. What you see in the family that raised the person you are dating, often times you will see again in them. They only know what they have been taught or raised to believe, until God is allowed in to **save, heal, deliver, and set free** by renewing the mind and changing the heart. Remember, you can't change them; only God can change a person's heart.

# Reflections:

## The Price I'm Willing to Pay?

If it was the dresses, stilettos, stockings, and long well-kept nails or the suits, ties, cologne, and romantic dates that captured the person into a relationship with you, it's going to take all of that and more to keep him or her.

If certain actions or words directed at you by the person you are dating are un-comfortable or rude, and you do not speak out in your own defense, it only nurtures this behavior to keep revisiting the relationship, until it gets out of control and overwhelming to you emotionally and/or physically.

If you witness uncontrollable anger early in the relationship and you ignore, downplay or deny its seriousness or think he/she will never use it against you, you are in for a great shock!

If you are disrespected in the beginning and you give it a pass, you will be giving more and more passes throughout the relationship.

In these types of relationships, individuals make an intentional decision to stay. What they are saying to everyone outside of the relationship is, "I'm willing to stay in this relationship to keep this person in my life" or "This is the price I'm willing to pay to maintain this relationship."

However, until marriage, single men and women should strive to please God by fulfilling their many purposes in life as they develop and maintain an intimate relationship with God. This relationship with God should consist of:

✓ Consistent prayer life

✓ Serving God's people

✓ Being a steward in the word of God

✓ Executing Kingdom principles

Pleasing God is much easier than pleasing mankind. Man changes: he or she will love you today and be in love with someone else tomorrow, but God never changes! His love, ordinances, and standards stay the same. Let's not pretend by trying to impress someone; be yourself in the relationship. Leave the games for children, and keep it real. Let the two of you learn and understand one another's ways and inclinations. When marriage does manifest, it will be a good, healthy marriage with true friendship and partnership that allow Christ to be the head.

Let your foundation be *the word of God, prayer, true love, faithfulness, trust*, and *communication*.

**Reflections:**

# *Chapter 2*

In this chapter

Dr. George discusses with you The BAR: being attentive and responsive in the relationship and its course!

CHAPTER – TWO

# THE BAR:

# Being Attentive and Responsive in the Relationship and its Course

Dating / Courtship

Imbalanced Relationships

Ungodly Soul Ties

When Violence Enters the Relationships

# Dating / Courtship

Is there a difference between dating and courtship?

Dating is defined as the activity of going on dates, the activity of going out regularly with somebody as a social or romantic partner.

Courtship is more intentional; it involves, trying to gain someone's love; it is the act of being attentive to someone with the expectation of developing a more intimate relationship. Courtship is like a prelude to marriage: it is the period of a romantic relationship before marriage.

Being wooed is also a way of defining courtship –most women enjoy being wooed or pursued by a man.

According to the above definitions, courtship can be seen as a platform between dating and marriage, where the couple has dated for a certain period of time and is now courting or is engaged, pursuing a profound understanding of one another. A couple's religious values and principles should align with their Christian faith; as well be the foundation upon which their relationship is built.

A biblical character who comes to mind named Jacob, really demonstrates the meaning of *wooing a woman,* as in his pursuit of Rachel. He set the value high for having Rachel as his wife, by offering her father his labor for seven years. Her father deceived Jacob, and Jacob extended his labor for an additional seven years; he was determined to have her as his wife *(Genesis 29th chapter)*. This action demonstrated the magnitude of her value to him. Jacob confirms for the man: (Proverbs 18:22) – New King James Version (NKJV)

*He who finds a wife finds a good thing, And obtains favor from the Lord.*

Jacob clearly gives illustrations to both man and woman. First to the man he illustrates how:

- He is to value and pursue a wife;
- He is to be dedicated and committed to his pursuit;
- He must see the value in having her in his life as his wife; and
- He must make the decision to work hard to win her love.

To the woman, he demonstrates the actions of a good man's pursuit. He reveals how a man will:

- See her value,
- Love her,
- Be faithful, and
- Be willing to work hard to win her love.

The favor of God was upon Jacob's life to receive the inheritance of Abraham, being of his seed. God also favored Jacob after he left his father-in-law's house with his two wives, children, servants, and livestock and headed back to his country where his brother made the promise to kill him, but did not because the Lord's favor spared his life.

Jacob illustrates that when you find the one for you, you must work to acquire her. The Bible does not say Rachel drummed up any schemes or tactics to trick Jacob in his pursuit of her. In Jacob's pursuit of Rachel, he was willing to do whatever it took to have her as his wife. He understood the value in having Rachel as his wife. He could have told her father he would work one year for him to have Rachel as his wife, but Jacob placed a high value on her worth by offering seven years of labor. A man must see the value in the one he chooses as his wife. This is true also for a woman: she must see value in the person who asks to have her as a wife, because once married she must submit and respect him as her head.

Value signifies treasure: when you treasure someone you love, you protect and respect the person's genuineness and worth. Jacob recognized this in Rachel. So, ladies –a man will work for you; you don't have to run after him; you don't have to buy him; you don't have to compete for him. He will see your value: just be yourself. Men, remember when you find the right one, you must see her value and be willing to work for her.

**Reflections:**

## Imbalanced Relationships

Being in relationships with unbelievers can cause devastating conflict, especially if they have different morals and values than those you live by. This conflict becomes tangible when two people begin to put forth efforts to please one another and the Christian in the relationship makes known his/her desire to also please God. In 2 Corinthians 6:14-18, Paul brings insight to this conflict. He writes:

**New King James Version** (NKJV)

14 Do not be unequally yoked together with unbelievers. For what fellowship has righteousness with lawlessness? And what communion has light with darkness?

15 And what accord has Christ with Belial? Or what part has a believer with an unbeliever?

16 And what agreement has the temple of God with idols? For you are the temple of the living God. As God has said: "I will dwell in them And walk among them. I will be their God, And they shall be My people."

17 Therefore "Come out from among them And be separate, says the Lord. Do not touch what is unclean, And I will receive you."

18 "I will be a Father to you, And you shall be My sons and daughters, Says the Lord Almighty."

One of the Greek definitions for unbelievers is without trust (in God).

When believers become involved in a dating relationship with unbelievers (as described in the scripture above), they position themselves to make poor choices in an effort to please the unbeliever. Paul asks a question that should incite the intellect of the believer: *what commonality has a believer with an unbeliever?* This is a good question, because how long will the Christian and the unbeliever go to sport games, dinners, and movies, which are all part of the **"impress you"** interlude of the relationship, before the two become combatants over their ethics, principles, and faith, engendering dissension in the relationship?

Many times the Christian in the relationship will separate from God before separating from the person causing the conflict in his or her relationship with God. When you separate from God *(because He never separates from you)*, you allow room for the enemy to move in. The more access you allow the enemy, the more you hear and listen to him. This is a BAR moment: learn to never ignore God's presence or call. When He comes, it's for a reason. He has something to say or impart unto you.

God has a time and season for everything we desire from him to manifest in our life. We have to understand the necessity of waiting on God's perfect timing for the things we have prayed for to enter our life.

Remember Sarah, Abraham's wife, when the angels of the Lord visited Abraham concerning Sodom's wickedness *(Genesis 18th chapter)*. Before the angels left, they said to Abraham (as Sarah listened in concealment), "I will surely return to you at this time next year (spring); and behold Sarah; your wife will have a son." God operates by time and seasons; He has a designated time and season for what you are waiting on to manifest in your life. Many times in your wait, it's for the merging of your proper season and God's timing, to achieve His divine plan instead of his permissive will for your life. God wants you to birth your heart's desire, not a miscarriage.

Many have failed to give birth to what God has placed in them; because they were unable to distinguish what was of God and what was not. A woman before she miscarries will look like she's about to give birth to life; sometimes she will feel like she's about to give birth to life, while at other times she can go through the delivery process like someone giving birth to life and yet produce death! God does not want your heart's desire to be aborted through a miscarriage; He wants it to have life!

**Reflection:**

## Ungodly Soul-Ties

The introduction of sex into the relationship of an un-married couple is one of the expeditious ways of developing **ungodly soul-ties**, although it's not the only way.
Soul ties can enter when there are no sexual relations involved,- just close associations, and we read in I Corinthians 15:33 that; "…bad company corrupts good character." (NLT) -

The definition of a "soul" is one of the human attributes that manifests as consciousness, thought, feelings, and will; it is regarded as distinct from the physical body.
In other words, it's your mind and heart that are very closely connected.
The word "tie" means to be attached, bound, joined or strapped together. "Ungodly" means disrespectful, wicked or sinful. To summarize the definition of an ungodly soul tie: **it's when minds and hearts are strapped, joined and bound to another in an ungodly relationship.**

I will share with you the case of an ungodly soul tie between a young single mother, who I will call Phyllis, and her baby's father, Richard. Phyllis is a struggling single female from a mixed ethnic background (half Caucasian and half African American). She is twenty-five years of age, with three children; ages two, eight and twelve. Phyllis was raised through the Kansas state child welfare system, moving from foster home to foster home.

The first time I met Phyllis, she expressed how lonely she felt and attributed some of her loneliness to not having a loving and supportive family. Throughout our conversations I felt her pain of loneliness, hopelessness, and fear. She expressed how she could barely make ends meet and had only one decent outfit to wear to work each day. Phyllis was a hard worker and a good provider for her children, in spite of the obstacle's she continued to face day after day.

Phyllis and her children moved to Chicago from Kansas City to follow the father of her two-year – old son. Phyllis does not have any relatives in Chicago, nor does she know anyone who lives here; her only motive for moving to Chicago was to follow what she believed to be love.

Someone who has not experienced true love (giving and receiving) can be vulnerable to receiving false love. False love is camouflaged with sweet words; uncomfortable feelings and heartrending acts develop in the relationship. These feelings and acts can range from unceasing disappointments to abusive behaviors. To really understand true love, one must come into an intimate relationship with the Trinity to experience:

➡ what is true love,
➡ how it's given, and
➡ the receiving of real love.

Those who have truly experienced true love have great insight in recognizing false love on sight.

Richard, the father of Phyllis's youngest son, is thirty-two years old, African American, unemployed, has only a high –school education, and lives with his mother. Phyllis has expressed her love for Richard and admits she will do anything to keep him in her life.

Phyllis and her children arrived in Chicago, receiving no financial or other support from Richard. They stayed in an emergency shelter until she found employment.  With a sales job at minimum wage, Phyllis was able to move them into a low –income community called Englewood. Phyllis was excited that; she was now able to bring some stability to her family. Having a one –bedroom apartment, she now was able to enroll her children in the community school.

 Phyllis knew her relationship with Richard was one –sided; she was in love with him, but he was not in love with her, and that was okay with her.  Richard only came around late at night to have sex and borrow money from her.  Now, mind you, Phyllis is no dummy: she is aware of what she is doing and she owns-up to the fact that Richard will probably never marry her.  She feels she can deal with this arrangement, because she is tired of being lonely and reminded of distresses and disappointments from previous relationships.

She is also aware he will never repay her any of the money he has borrowed, but just the thought that she will have him all to herself for that small amount of time was worth it to her.  Phyllis stated how she looked forward to the late –night calls from Richard or his surprise visits; she said this made her feel he was at least thinking of her.

One day, as Phyllis was sharing a painful situation that had taken place, tears began to slide down her pale little cheeks. She dropped her head and lay her hands across her chest and said she and Richard had broken up.

This was not the first time she'd broken –up with Richard; each time, a couple of days later, guess who stopped by or called with a sad story?

Phyllis shared that just when she believed she had gotten over him, he would show up with a distressing story that would draw her back into his clutches and the cycle would begin again, repeating itself over and over again.  She likened this feeling to being sucked back into a hypnotic, addictive relationship that she wished so hard to be free of: -in her mind, heart, and body!

Ungodly soul ties are dangerous; they can be *demanding, manipulative,* and *addictive.* You feel *trapped, knitted, tied,* and *bound* to the person.  Your mind will never seem to take rest from them.  Always thinking of ways to please them, desiring to be with them, craving to be held or touched by them, you will lose complete focus on God and self; it becomes all about them and what makes them happy.

Although Phyllis was in an ungodly soul tie with Richard, she had the qualities to become free. Phyllis had several strengths in her favor; she was:

- A hard worker,
- A good provider,
- Resourceful, and
- A self-motivator.

Phyllis's strengths included her ability to move to a large city knowing no one and obtain a place for her children and herself to live. She found employment, and an apartment and enrolled her children in school. Her weakness was succumbing to loneliness; she didn't know self or how to please or enjoy self. She didn't value her worth. With an introduction to the Lord, good counseling, a great mentor/life coach, and assistance from several social support systems/agencies, Phyllis was placed on a course leading her to her passion in life.

Many times people like Phyllis need to know someone is there to support them and be the cushion in case of a fall. This was Phyllis's case: she needed someone to encourage her, point out her strengths and show her how to use them to her advantage. As for the healing of hurtful wounds she received only the Holy Spirit and her relationship with Him can heal those areas in her life, but the separation from Richard must be done by her.

# Reflections:

## How to avoid ungodly soul-ties?

This is a BAR moment: First, understand this happens to both men and women. Know there are hunters out there who study and prey on vulnerable people like Phyllis.
Before you commit to a relationship, the two of you, must:

➡ Jointly identify and agree in the beginning on the type of relationship you will have.

➡ Not give more than the relationship calls for; there should be 50/50 give-and-take for both.

➡ Learn to set boundaries. Do not give someone you are not married to too much information or access to you and your time.

Equipping someone with too much information about you only gives them ammunition to use against you, especially if their intentions are not good to begin with. This places them behind the control panels of your mind and emotions, and guess who will be controlled and manipulated in the relationship? You will also become the injured victim in the relationship.

**Reflections:**

## When Violence Enters the Relationship

Every relationship has it stresses, but when violence is carried into the relationship, the possibility of fatality heightens for both individuals, and those connected to them, such as children and immediate family members.

Statistics state that about 85 percent of women are more likely than men to become victims of violence in an intimate relationship. One in every four women will experience domestic violence in her lifetime. In *2005 1,181 women in the United States were murdered* by an intimate partner. That's an average of three women every day. Of all the women murdered in the United States about *one-third were killed by their intimate partner.* Domestic violence can be defined as a pattern of abusive behavior in any relationship that is used by one person to gain or maintain power and control over an intimate partner. According to the National Center for Injury Prevention and Control, women experience about 4.8 million intimate partner-related physical assaults and rapes every year. Less than 20 percent of battered women sought medical treatment following an injury. According to the *National Crime Victimization Survey*, which includes crimes that were not reported to the police, *232,960 women in the United States were raped* or sexually assaulted in 2006. That's more than 600 women every day.
A significant number of crimes are never reported for reasons that include the victim's feeling that nothing can or will be done and the personal nature of the incident.

I had a friend in high school, who I will call Dawn. We were very close friends: we loved to laugh, shop, and act silly as we shared our dreams with one another, like most teenagers, and believe me, we were big dreamers! We promised one another to never allow a man to hit or beat on us; it was an oath between two friends.

After graduating from high school, I left for college while Dawn stayed in Chicago and continued in the workforce. During my college years, we didn't stay in regular touch with one another, but after graduation, upon my returning home, our friendship rekindled. We partied, double-dated, and shopped till we dropped! I was a new comer to driving so Dawn took many daring risks riding with me. I remember one day when driving west bound on 111th street in Chicago, I accidently made a right turn onto the ramp of an expressway *(I-57).* Mind you, I had never driven on an expressway and I was petrified. Dawn trusted my driving more than I did; she thought it was hilarious. She laughed, laughed, laughed and I screamed, screamed, screamed until I reached the very next exit.

As we became older and wiser, we took life more seriously and pursued better jobs that drew us in different directions in life. In 1978 I accepted Jesus Christ into my life; the more I pursued a closer relationship with Christ the more my interest in life changed. Several years passed where Dawn and I didn't communicate much with one another, mostly due to our dissimilar interest now.

About five years later, I met a mutual friend of ours, who I will call Shirley. Shirley lived next door to Dawn.  Dawn had always had an apartment and had lived alone since high-school graduation.  When I asked Shirley if she had seen Dawn lately, her reply was "yes, especially when the police come by, and you know she has a son now."  I asked Shirley "what do you mean when the police come by?"  I also didn't know Dawn had a child, so this was a surprise also, but the police were a greater surprise. Shirley explained how Dawn had a friend living with her and they fought often, especially on weekends.  I thought to myself "oh no!" The memory of our promise to one another came back to mind.  Shirley said the fights would become pretty bad, but Dawn would never have him arrested; every time the policemen arrived she would say "I'm alright."  Shirley continued, lowering her head toward the ground, as she said she and the neighbors, continued to call the police when they heard the fights.

I was so hurt; although we had made this promise to one another I never really believed either of us would be in this type of situation.  I immediately began to pray for Dawn; my prayer was for her to get out of the relationship.  I was not educated about domestic violence, but I just knew I could save my friend, so I called her and asked what was going on.  She described everything as being okay; and never mentioned anything relating to what Shirley had spoken of, so I didn't press.  I decided to just hang around more and see for myself.  I finally received the opportunity to meet this friend of hers, who had moved in and fathered her son. He was about 5'10" nicely built, bow legged and somewhat attractive. He worked in a factory and made a decent salary.  He drove a drop – top red corvette and had lived previously with his sister and her family.  Dawn's friend drank beer and partied on weekends, but worked every day during the week. He appeared to think much of himself, maybe even too much. One day while visiting Dawn, I observed that she was nervous around him and somewhat insecure, so I kept my comments and opinion of him to myself and pretended to know nothing of the fights and altercations with the police.

One day Dawn called me from her place of employment; to tell me she and her friend had broken up. Well, I thought, this is it, thank God!  Overly excited about my friend finally becoming free of this person whom I portrayed as a coward, I said to Dawn GOOD! I heard he was hitting on you and why did you allow it, we made a promise to one another we would never allow a man to hit us; what happened, Dawn?
Dawn became very quiet on the telephone; she didn't say a word and a second or two later, she began to stutter and said, "I have to get back to work. I'll talk to you later."  Well, as you probably can imagine, that conversation never happened.  I would call and she was either too busy to talk or was never there, and if I left messages for her, she never returned them.

I lost my friend due to my lack of knowledge about domestic violence.  This haunted me for years until I finally did something about it.  I pursued proper training in working with victims of domestic violence. During my training, I learned the most dangerous time is when a woman is leaving her abuser, and it takes approximately seven attempts before she actually leaves. I also learned that counseling her was not like counseling someone who has just broken up with her boyfriend. There is much patience, compassion, support (physical and mental), and encouragement that needs to be given to her. This woman, regardless of who she was before this relationship or how strong she once was, is now programmed to think less of herself. What once was her strength has become fear; she feels powerless to succeed in anything she may desire to accomplish. She has become trained to depend totally upon her abuser, even to gain or maintain anything of value.

Over the many years of training, what I found most intriguing about victims of domestic violence was why they stayed. This is what I didn't take into consideration with Dawn, nor did I consider her options, if there were any in her mind. She had a small child and made an okay salary, but psychologically she was not the Dawn I once knew.

Dawn didn't have any siblings, she was an only child with no aunts or uncles in Chicago, and her parents divorced right after Dawn graduated from high school. She didn't feel she had any support from either parent; they both were involved in their new lives and new families. Dawn was barely making ends meet to support herself, but now she had a child, an apartment, and the up-keep of an automobile. I'm sure this was great pressure on her mind, making her wonder if she could do this alone. Knowing Dawn, she probably felt she could not make it without her friend's help and he may have assured her of this many times. Her friend probably viewed her vulnerabilities: -lack of parental and family support, being financially limited, having a small child, and being deeply in love with him –as an opportunity for him to take advantage of her; it was probably a relationship he was able to easily manipulate to his benefit.

This is a "Bar" moment women have to watch for, by staying attentive and responsive in the relationship and its course. We must look beyond today and see what next week, next month, or possibly next year could look like in the relationship. There are times when we, as women, feel the relationship is definitely aiming in a certain direction and surrender our heart/will to the other person in the relationship. Dangerous, ladies, this is dangerous! This is where the enemy places blinders on your eyes, and you see only what he wants you to see versus the actuality of the relationship. God will send red flags and himself, but you must be willing to see and hear God when he comes.

Ladies, you must set boundaries in the relationship; if you don't, he will, and the boundaries he sets may not be to your advantage, but to his. The next thing you know, your "ideal relationship" has become a terrifying experience!

## Who are the batters?

Men who batter women come from all socioeconomic backgrounds, races, religions, and walks of life. The abuser may be a blue-collar or white-collar worker, unemployed or highly paid.  He may be a drinker or non-drinker.  The batterer may be a good father, a good provider, a sober and upstanding member of the community, and an active member of his religious congregation.  He may be charming and outgoing; however, men who abuse often share certain common traits.  These include jealousy and possessiveness; they have a tendency to minimize and deny the abuse.  They can have traditional beliefs about the roles of men and women; a belief that violence is a man's right and should not be challenged.

## Who are the victims?

A battered woman might be the vice president at your local bank, your child's Sunday – school teacher, your beautician, your dentist, your pastor's wife or the person who clears your table at the restaurant where you have lunch.  She may be a well-educated professional or unable to read.  She may be Christian, Jewish, Catholic, or Muslim, or she may have no strong religious beliefs.  She may be a new immigrant with limited English skills.  She may be a newlywed, or have just celebrated her golden wedding anniversary. In other words, she could be anyone.

Battering can also occur in same-gender relationships, which is an especially difficult situation because there is often no safe place to which the victims can turn.  We must remember that children who experience or observe violence in their homes are also victims, and this is a learned behavior.

There has been violence against women as far back as biblical times:

- Dinah, the daughter of Jacob and Leah, was sexually assaulted by Shechem a Hivite. Because he was attracted to her he decided he wanted her, so he took her by force and made her commit a sexual act that she did not want to be a part of. *(Genesis 34:1-31)*.

- David's son, Amnon raped his half-sister Tamar, who was also David's daughter. *(II Samuel 13 and 14 Chapter)*.

Sexual violence against women has existed as far back as ancient biblical times. What is happening today is nothing new, but what has changed are the consequences for the perpetrator.  If victims do not report the crime committed against them, they feel powerless, defeated, and angry. Instead of harboring this negative energy inside you, put it to good use and stand up for yourself; you deserve it!

# FORMS OF ABUSE

## PHYSICAL ABUSE

- Pushes or shoves you
- Holds you to keep you from leaving
- Slaps or bites you
- Kicks or chokes you
- Hits or punches you
- Throws objects at you
- Locks you out of the house
- Abandons you in dangerous places
- Refuses to help when you are sick
- Rapes you
- Threatens or hurts you with a weapon

## SEXUAL ABUSE

- Treats women as sex objects
- Exhibits jealousy and/or anger and assumes you would have sex with any available partner
- Insists you dress in a more sexual way than you want
- Minimizes the importance of your feelings about sex
- Criticizes you sexually
- Insists on unwanted and uncomfortable touching
- Withholds sex and affection
- Calls you sexual names like "whore" and "frigid"
- Forces you to strip when you do not want to
- Publicly shows interest in other women
- Has affairs with other women after agreeing to a monogamous relationship
- Forces you to have sex with him or others or forces you to watch others have sex
- Forces particular unwanted sexual acts upon you

➢ Forces you to have sex after physically assaulting you

➢ Forces you to have sex when your health is in jeopardy

➢ Forces you to have sex for the purpose of hurting you with objects or weapons

➢ Commits sadistic sexual acts

## EMOTIONAL ABUSE

➢ Ignores your feelings

➢ Ridicules or insults women as a group

➢ Ridicules or insults your most valued beliefs: religion, race, heritage, or class

➢ Withholds approval, appreciation, or affection as punishment

➢ Continually criticizes you, calls you names, or shouts at you

➢ Insults or drives away your friends or family

➢ Withholds money or coerces you to turn over control of your money to him or her

➢ Is irresponsible with marital debt, ruining your credit

➢ Isolates you from family, friends, and community

➢ Threatens your family members with physical injury

➢ Humiliates you in private or public

➢ Refuses to socialize with you

➢ Takes car keys away from you

➢ Regularly threatens to leave you or tells you to leave

➢ Threatens to kidnap the children when he is angry at you

➢ Abuses pets to hurt you

➢ Accuses you of having affairs

➢ Manipulates you with lies and contradictions

# ABUSE CHECKLIST

Look over the following questions. Think about how you are being treated and how you treat your partner. Remember: when one person *scares, hurts, or continually puts down the other person, its abuse.*

### *Does your partner…*

✓ Embarrass or make fun of you in front of your friends or family?

✓ Put down your accomplishments or goals?

✓ Make you feel like you are unable to make decisions?

✓ Use intimidation or threats to gain compliance?

✓ Tell you that you are nothing without him or her?

✓ Treat you roughly –grab, push, pinch, AND SHOVE or hit you?

✓ Call you several times a night or show up to make sure you are where you said you would be?

✓ Use drugs or alcohol as an excuse for saying hurtful things or abusing you?

✓ Blame you for how he or she feel or act?

✓ Pressure you sexually for things you aren't ready for?

✓ Make you feel there is "no way out" of the relationship?

✓ Prevent you from doing things you want—like spending time with your friends or family?

✓ Try to keep you from leaving after a fight or leave you somewhere after a fight to "teach you a lesson"

Although I lost Dawn and was not able to reach her, through the help of God, I pray to never mishandle another victim of domestic violence. I see Dawn in every woman or man I meet who is a victim. With each victim I help, I remember the mistake I made with Dawn and that motivates me to do all I can to assist the "Dawn's" that enter my life!

My aspiration is to educate the Christian community about the "Dawn's" that are sitting in their pews today; I fulfill this through workshops I facilitate, titled **"I'M SITTING IN YOUR PEW."** I beseech the church: please do not mishandle her; she's too delicate, too fragile, and can easily be broken into millions of precious pieces that can be so challenging to put back together again.

*IF YOU NEE HELP Please Call:*

THE NATIONAL DOMESTIC VIOLENCE HOTLINE AT 1-800-799-7233
THE NATIONAL SEXUAL ASSAULT HOTLINE AT 1-800-656-4673
THE NATIONAL TEEN DATING ABUSE HOTLINE AT 1-866-331-9474

**Reflections:**

# *Chapter 3*

In this chapter Dr.
George teaches on the
Sexuality of "Man"

CHAPTER – THREE

# The Sexuality of "Man"

Made in the Image of God

The Desire Factor

Transferring spirits through sexual relations

# Made In the Image of God

New King James Version (NKJV)

26 Then God said, "Let Us make man in Our image, according to Our likeness; let them have dominion over the fish of the sea, over the birds of the air, and over the cattle, over all the earth and over every creeping thing that creeps on the earth."

27 So God created man in His own image; in the image of God He created him; male and female He created them.

*Genesis 1:26-27*

The Message (MSG)

26 God spoke: "Let us make human beings in our image, make them reflect our nature So they can be responsible for the fish in the sea, the birds in the air, the cattle, And, yes, Earth itself, and every animal that moves on the face of Earth."

27 God created human beings; he created them godlike, Reflecting God's nature. He created them male and female.

Genesis 1:26-27

## A human being consists of three parts:

- Spirit                        *John 4:24*
- Mind/soul                *Ephesians 4:30, John 14:26, 16:13*
- Body                        *John 1:14*

## As explained in 1Thessalonians 5:23:

New King James Version (NKJV)

23 Now may the God of peace Himself sanctify you completely; and may your whole spirit, soul, and body be preserved blameless at the coming of our Lord Jesus Christ.

The Message (MSG)

23 May God himself, the God who makes everything holy and whole, make you holy and whole, put you together - spirit, soul, and body - and keep you fit for the coming of our Master, Jesus Christ.

## In the gospels, we see many of Jesus's emotions expressed:

- Compassion:        *John 8:1-12*
- Indignation:        *Matthew 21:12*
- Sorrow:                *John 11th chapter*
- Frustration:        *Mark 4:38-41*

Jesus expressed deep emotions as He walked this earth, and we must never be afraid to reveal our true feelings to Him. He understands your emotions, for He experienced them also when He walked this earth:

New King James Version (NKJV)

15 For we do not have a High Priest who cannot sympathize with our weaknesses, but was in all points tempted as we are, yet without sin.
Hebrews 4:15

The Message (MSG)

15 We don't have a priest who is out of touch with our reality. He's been through weakness and testing, and experienced it all - all but the sin.
Hebrews 4:15


Be honest and do not try to conceal anything from your saviour. He's an omniscient God; He knows all things; He cares for you and everything concerning you.
We have the ability to reflect His character in our *love, patience, forgiveness, kindness,* and *faithfulness*. Knowing we are made in God's image and share many of his characteristics provides a solid basis for self-worth.

Human worth is not based on possessions, achievements, physical attractiveness, or public acclaim. Instead, it is based on being made in God's image. Since we bear God's image, we can feel positive about ourselves. Criticizing or downgrading self is criticizing what God has made and the abilities He has given you. Knowing that you are a person of worth helps you love God, know Him personally, and make a valuable contribution to those around you.

# Reflections:

# The Desire Factor

Not understanding the consequences attached to forbidden sexual union between two unmarried individuals has ramifications that can result in emotional and spiritual distress, for both male and female. Everything we need to learn about self, relationships, and God points back to the beginning in Genesis. Adam and Eve disobeyed God's instructions while living in the Garden (Genesis 3:1-7). God chastised both individuals, but we are highlighting Eve's reprimand:

New King James Version (NKJV)
16 To the woman He said: "I will greatly multiply your sorrow and your conception; In pain you shall bring forth children; Your desire shall be for your husband, And he shall rule over you."
Genesis 3:16

The Message (MSG)
16 He told the woman: "I'll multiply your pains in childbirth; you'll give birth to your babies in pain. You'll want to please your husband, but he'll lord it over you."
Genesis 3:16

When God placed Adam and Eve together, He instituted marriage. When the Bible gives reference to sex between a man and woman, it's referring to a husband and his wife, who are married to each other, unless it is pointing out sin. God's chastisement of woman was to multiply her sorrow in child bearing, give her desire for her husband, and give the husband power over her.
I want to focus on the second part of this chastisement, which is the *desire factor*, HER DESIRE FOR HER HUSBAND. The Hebrew word for DESIRE in this verse is tshuwqah, its Hebrew meaning is: to long after, crave for, and run after. Woman will desire and yearn for her husband; this desire is broader than simply sex, but it does not exclude the sexual element.

Before the fall in the garden, Adam and Eve experienced true intimacy with one another, which was a divine love. The Bible said Adam cleaved to his wife-Genesis 2:24. This means he left everyone else and clung to Eve. He kept her by his side; he pursued her, frequently joined himself to her, followed her around, and stayed with her. Adam was working to keep Eve's interest in him. She did not have to pursue him for attention or affection. She did not have to run after him or look for him to bring him back to the garden; he was home every night, and he kept the romance in their marriage fervent. Eve didn't have to ask if he loved her; she knew he did, because Adam demonstrated his love for her through his actions. Adam wasn't knocking her up-side her head, calling her all kind of "B's" and spitting on her.

Remember, when Adam first laid eyes on Eve, he said *"This is now bone of my bones, and flesh of my flesh: she shall be called Woman, because she was taken out of Man."* Adam recognized Eve being a part of him, they are one; he recognized the value in having Eve and handled her as so. He was so amused and approving of Eve and the fact that she was all his that he expressed this by calling her "bone of my bones, …flesh of my flesh." He named her woman, which means *wife;* he didn't give her the name Eve, meaning *life or living*, until after the fall when their intimacy was broken due to their sin.

Eve was accustomed to a certain way Adam approached, related, and responded to her; she was acquainted with him as being affectionate and attentive to her and her needs. The "DESIRE FACTOR" is God's reason for conditions in relationships to exist after the fall, because the intimacy that was once shared between the first man and his wife will not be the same.

This intimacy, where a man and a woman who are married to one another become "one," was designed and appointed by God. When the Bible speaks of a husband, it is speaking of a man married to a woman; this man and woman should only experience sexual oneness with one another. A sexual tie or bond can affect a person *physically, emotionally,* and *spiritually;* that's why a husband and wife become one when consummation takes place in the marriage. According to the above scripture, the Hebrew meaning for the word "DESIRE" says the wife's love for her husband will stretch out for him as to run after him, she will continuously long for his affections and he will rule over her. The word "rule" itself has diverse meanings such as to govern, decide, and exercise dominion and control over someone or something.

This same decree presents itself to the single man and woman who are not married and engage in sexual relations (fornication) with one another. It does not change because the two are not married. This unmarried woman puts herself in a very vulnerable position, where she can experience the same emotions as a married woman, where she will long after the man with whom she has become *"one"* or sexually intimate; she will at times crave his love and affections and even pursue him.

Sex is profound and has a powerful influence on one's mind, spirit, and body. Woman's desire for man is an attraction that cannot be uprooted from her nature. Paul never commanded the wife to love her husband; he knew that "desire" would manifest after consummation of the marriage. He said:

"Husbands, love your wives, even as Christ also loved the church, and gave himself for it,"- *Ephesians 5:25 (KJV). He's telling him how deep and committed his love is to be for his wife.*

"So ought men to love their wives as their own bodies. He that loveth his wife loveth himself," *Ephesians 5:28 (KJV). He is to take care of her, protect her physically and emotionally.*

"Husbands, love your wives, and be not bitter against them," *Colossians 3:19 (KJV). He's telling him how he is to relate to his wife.*

However, Paul instructed the woman to succumb to her husband:
"Wives, submit yourselves unto your <u>own husbands</u>, as unto the Lord,"
*Ephesians 5:22 (KJV). She is to be committed and faithful to her husband.* Why did Paul say to the woman, submit to your own husband?
"Wives, submit yourselves unto your own husbands, as it is fit in the Lord," *Colossians 3:18 (KJV). She is to respect and honor her husband.*

Paul never instructed the wife to love her husband because God placed the "DESIRE FACTOR" in her as far back as the garden: "…and thy desire shall be to thy husband………" *Genesis 3:16, (KJV).*

A man and a woman both need to feel loved; just as a man needs to feel honored and respected. A woman need to feel external affections and security, God created them so. When man and woman are united as one in intimacy, there will be expressions in her that will long after, stretch out, and crave for his affections. That's why this type of relationship is for married couples, not the un-married. Something happens to a woman when she joins sexually with a man and, yes, he will have power over her sometimes and even control, especially in the emotional realm. God designed and structured the family to be as such: where Christ submits to God, man submits to Christ, and woman submits to man. The love Christ displays for the church is to be exhibited through this union and marriage of a man and his wife.

How many times have we observed a woman who is not married to a man but is involved sexually with him, as she physically and financially provides for him, usually just to keep him in her life, as Phyllis revealed through her story?
Many times if he leaves, she will go after him or will always take him back –why? She has joined herself with this man in a morally forbidden way. According to the word of God, the effect of being *"one"* is that she will experience the "DESIRE FACTOR"-*longing, pursuing, and craving for his love and attention.* That's what keeps her wanting and desiring him; the intimacy that she participated in has now produced these affections in her for him.

"……..and he shall rule over thee." This statement can manifest physically or psychologically for the woman, where the man will have influences over her emotions and actions. Being unmarried and involved in a sexual relationship causes her to struggle with emotional wounds and insecurities within herself, especially if the relationship is one-sided, where she is in love but he's not, as the case was with Phyllis.

For the woman a morally forbidden union is usually demoralizing *spiritually, psychologically, and physically.* We, as women, must think about this: if Paul had to remind the married man to love his wife, who took an oath before God to promise to love and honor his wife till death do them a part, what makes the unmarried woman believe the man she is sleeping with and not married to will be mindful of her heart and feelings and commit his love to her? Remember, Jacob worked hard for Rachel.

If the man really respects and, loves you and wants to protect your honor, he will not be full of excuses, but will marry you before having sex with you. He will not be full of false promises of "wait or we'll do it later" and later becomes five, six, or ten years later and you're still not married. He will do whatever it takes to get you and keep you, because he sees the value in having you as his wife!

**Reflections:**

## Transferring of Spirits

Are we so mindful of who lay hands on us more than who we intimately lie down with and join our-self to as one?

New King James Version (NKJV)
16 Or do you not know that he who is joined to a harlot is one body with her? For "the two," He says, "shall become one flesh."
17 But he who is joined to the Lord is one spirit with Him.
18 Flee sexual immorality. Every sin that a man does is outside the body, but he who commits sexual immorality sins against his own body.
19 Or do you not know that your body is the temple of the Holy Spirit who is in you, whom you have from God, and you are not your own?
1 Corinthians 6:16-19

The Message (MSG)
16 There's more to sex than mere skin on skin. Sex is as much spiritual mystery as physical fact. As written in Scripture, "The two become one."
17 Since we want to become spiritually one with the Master, we must not pursue the kind of sex that avoids commitment and intimacy, leaving us more lonely than ever - the kind of sex that can never "become one."
18 There is a sense in which sexual sins are different from all others. In sexual sin we violate the sacredness of our own bodies, these bodies that were made for God-given and God-modeled love, for "becoming one" with another.
19 Or didn't you realize that your body is a sacred place, the place of the Holy Spirit? Don't you see that you can't live however you please; squandering what God paid such a high price for? The physical part of you is not some piece of property belonging to the spiritual part of you.
1 Corinthians 6:16-19

Look at Paul's words of wisdom to the Corinthians above. When the two became one in body, not only did they commit sexual sin, but also take into account the transferring of spirits they shared during this act. When we lie intimately with another person, there is a transferring of spirits; fluid is one of the catalysts of travel for spirits. You have become intimate not only with this individual, but also with other individuals they have been intimate with. If they have any sexually transmitted diseases from others, so do you!

Paul validates our battle with spirits enlightening us with the true meaning of spiritual warfare:

New King James Version (NKJV)

12 For we do not wrestle against flesh and blood, but against principalities, against powers, against the rulers of the darkness of this age, against spiritual hosts of wickedness in the heavenly places.
(Ephesians 6:12)

The Message (MSG)

12 This is no afternoon athletic contest that we'll walk away from and forget about in a couple of hours. This is for keeps, a life-or-death fight to the finish against the Devil and all his angels.
(Ephesians 6:12)

Being on the receiving end of such attacks, one will wonder how and why? Your involvement in sin and ungodly soul ties can separate you from God so that you become vulnerable to the schemes and attacks of the enemy. It's through forbidden sexual acts and corrupt associations: (…evil communications corrupt good manners- 1 Corinthians 15:33), that doors are opened for Satan's plots to be activated through you.

Spirits need a body to act out and fulfill their desires. They attach to and oppress others to open doors unto them; their sole purpose is to gain entrance to control, fulfill, and exhibit their desires through your body.

**Illustration:**

You commit sin by having sexual intercourse with a woman or man that is not your husband or wife, and this person is currently being oppressed by the spirit of lust. By committing this moral sin, you have opened a door or entrance for such spirit (lust) to attach, oppress, and manipulate actions through you.

The man and woman have entered into a forbidden sexual act that is part of an establishment instituted by God for a husband and his wife. If the two are not married to one another, they have committed a sexual sin before God.

There are consequences for practicing this sin, which is categorized in one of the works of the flesh. The seventeen works of the flesh are: *adultery, fornication, uncleanness, lasciviousness, idolatry, witchcraft, hatred, variance, emulations, wrath, strife, seditions, heresies, envying, murders, drunkenness,* and *reveling*, and they that do such things shall not inherit the kingdom of God- Galatians' 5: 19-21.

## Reflections:

# *Chapter 4*

Did you know a constant desire for physical love and seeking assurance of one's self-worth are symptoms of rejection?

CHAPTER – FOUR

# EMOTIONAL HEALING

Emotions/Feelings

Psychological Weapons

Rejection

Dynamics of Fear

Anger

Self-worth

## Emotions/Feelings

Emotions involve strong or heightened feelings about someone or something. Feelings are closely related to your thinking, and thinking certain thoughts can produce positive or negative emotions. Motivation is another aspect to emotions, where biological stimulation of certain emotions can motivate us to act certain ways.

POSITIVE EMOTIONS: joy, tenderness, love, peace, boldness, excitement, surprise, and strength.

NEGATIVE EMOTIONS: sadness, anxiety, fear, anger, stress, depression, rejection, guilt, insecurities, and loneliness.

Emotional wounds occur when an individual's feelings and mind *(thinking)* have been injured through unhealthy relationships. The following is a list of feelings we experience on a day-to-day basis through our interactions with one another. These feelings can grow to become emotional scars/injuries, exposing a need for inner healing in our life. They have caused hindrances' –in our Christian and social growth and maturity.

➡ **UNFORGIVENESS**: reluctance to forgive someone for the wrong they have done. Is it hard for you to forgive yourself or others?

➡ **ANXIETY**: abnormal and overwhelming sense of fear (psychological signs can include sweating, tension and increased pulse rate). Are you fearful of people, new relationships or performances required of you?

➡ **ANGER**: rage, fury (destructive rage), and indignation (anger aroused by something unjust). Do you find yourself lashing out at others or exhibiting sudden outbursts of anger, hate, or resentment?

➡ **INFERIORITY**: viewing one's self-value as of little or less importance than that of another. Do you always see others more positively than you do yourself in looks and/ or performances?

➡ **REDUCED OR DESTROYED SELF-ESTEEM**: low to no self- confidence/satisfaction. Is it hard for you to see anything good or positive in self?

➡️ **REJECTION**: feeling refused unaccepted, unconsidered, thrown back, or declined. Do you find it hard to love or like self?

➡️ **LONELINESS**: feeling without company and sad from being lonely. Do you often find yourself alone and sad, even in a crowd? Do you find it hard to mingle with others?

➡️ **OLD HURTS AND WOUNDS**: to have ones feelings hurt in the past and never healed of such wounds. Do you experience painful feelings that seem to never leave?

➡️ **PAST EMBARRASSING PAIN**: having been painfully embarrassed in the past and continually experiencing that pain. Have you experienced a humiliating moment, the memory of which continues to reoccur in your mind?

➡️ **INADEQUACY**: feeling insufficient in comparison to others. Do you often (negatively) compare yourself to others?

➡️ **SENSITIVITY**: being easily hurt emotionally, delicately aware of the attitudes and feelings of others. Are you often crying and sad over simple things in life?

➡️ **GUILT**: constantly believing that you have committed an offense. Do you constantly feel sad and remorseful over something you have apologized for?

➡️ **STRESS**: feeling strain and/or tension in the body/mind. Do you often feel overwhelmed, and irritable?

➡️ **DEPRESSION**: feeling sad, in low spirits, having difficulty with thinking and concentrating. Have you experienced periods of feeling gloomy, dejected, and hopeless?

➡️ **WORRY**: being anxious. mentally distressed, or tormented to the point of destroying peace of mind. Have you agonized over a constant feeling of uneasiness, heavy burden, and fearfulness?

➡ **SHAME**: experiencing feelings of dishonor, unworthiness, and embarrassment. Have you suffered feelings of disgrace and humiliation?

➡ **HOSTILITY**: being unfriendly in relation to an enemy, opposition, or resistance. Do you exhibit aggression, resentment or intimidation toward someone in particular?

**Reflections:**

## Psychological Weapons

Some of the most powerful weapons in Satan's armory are psychological. Most commonly used are *fear, doubt, anger, hostility, worry, low self-esteem,* and of course *guilt* and *shame*. Long-standing guilt and shame are hard to shake off; they seem to hang on, even after the Christian claims forgiveness and accepts God's pardoning grace. An uneasy sense of self-condemnation hangs over many Christians. They often find themselves defeated by these powerful psychological weapons that Satan uses.

Many of God's people are in a psychological war, but do not realize it. This war is taking place on the battle-ground of their minds and in the emotional realm. They find themselves struggling with mental confusion and painful memories, unable to separate themselves from a negative past and uncontrollable thoughts and acts. This war is a product of the heart –wrenching injuries they endured in unhealthy relationships. Such relationships have left many so emotionally and psychologically wounded that they have become stagnated, unable to move forward in life. These injuries of the heart and mind require the work of the Holy Spirit to heal. Such healing will stimulate a rewarding transformation in how one values self, mentally and emotionally. This transformation sculpts them to become the man or woman God intended them to be. Such renewal permits them to recognize and pursue healthy relationships that will add to them and not subtract from them. They are able to distinguish love from lust, realizing that love gives and lust takes away.

Most emotionally wounded individuals can recognize something is uncharacteristic about them and may feel as if they are "losing it." They become isolated and do not share what they are experiencing, for fear of appearing different or strange to others, not realizing that many share the same experiences. What has happened is that Satan took a page from his ancient play book; using new players, he is tapping into their minds or psyches to feed them negative information about their –self, and they are believing it.

Satan tried to use this same play on Job, through Job's wife (Job 2:10), as one of his enforcers. Remember, Satan uses the same old play book, just different players, and it didn't work. Job didn't fall for the message Satan was sending him through his wife; Job told his wife, "You talk like a foolish woman!" We never heard from her anymore –just that God blessed Job with twice as much as he had before.

This is what the enemy is doing with many who have been injured emotionally through unhealthy relationships. If the enemy can isolate you as he feeds you negative thoughts and experiences he has exaggerated or fabricated, he will generate psychological struggles within your mind. These struggles are designed with the intent of controlling and manipulating you to believe what he, Satan, is planting in your mind, which will produce doubt, fear, and a sense of low self-worth and/or inferiority toward others.

The enemy torments the mind with negative experiences you suffered or very painful memories of your past. There are also times when the enemy will bring people into your life for the express purpose of producing negative conditions or occurrences. These negative circumstances can be:

- Rejection, self-rejection

- Sin: fornication, adultery, lust, idolatry, occults, etc.

- Abuse: physical, emotional or sexual

- Grief

- Doubt, rebellion and disobedience to God

- Crime: rape, violence

- Addictions: substance, alcohol or food

- Painful childhood memories

- Shame/guilt

- Unhealthy relationships

And the list goes on. When the enemy uses such devices including doubt, anger, and worry, it leaves the individual feeling insecure –battling one or several of the following emotions, but not limited to:

- Low self-image

- Anxieties

- Depression/hate

- Rage/violence/bitterness

- Fears

- Inferiority complex

- Stress

- Over sensitivity/isolation

- Nervousness/paranoid

**Reflections:**

# Rejection

"FOR AS HE THINKETH IN HIS HEART, SO IS HE….,"
PROVERBS 23:7 (KJV).

Immobilization travels on the path of rejection. Rejection has a number of disclosures and a variety of ways of representing itself. It can be purposely or unintentionally given or imagined. Whether active or passive, real or imaginary, it robs Jesus Christ of His rightful Lordship in the life of God's children, and it robs God's people of the vitality and quality of life God intended for them. John 10:10 addresses this:

*"the thief cometh not, but for to steal, and to kill, and to destroy: i am come that they might have life, and that they might have it more abundantly."*

Rejection may begin at any time, from the time of conception until death; like many physical illnesses, its symptoms may not be perceived immediately. Many people are unaware they have suffered from its effects until they are freed from them.

Rejection may be received by the manner or time of conception,-for instance: children conceived out of wedlock; in anger; as a result of rape, incest, adultery; or from a drug-dependent relationship. Many may experience signs of rejection from birth onward: children born to parents who did not want them, who may be considered a strain on the family budget; the last of a large family; and, strangely, the middle child in a family often struggle with rejection. Rejection may be received in a mother's womb:

*".... The Lord has called me from the womb; from the matrix of my mother He has made mention of my name." (Isaiah 49:1).*

New King James Version (NKJV)

4 Then the word of the Lord came to me, saying:

5 "Before I formed you in the womb I knew you; Before you were born I sanctified you; I ordained you a prophet to the nations."

(Jeremiah 1:4-5)

New King James Version (NKJV)

13 For You formed my inward parts; You covered me in my mother's womb.

(Psalms 139:13)

The circumstances surrounding a pregnant woman and her attitude toward her unborn child influence the child in her uterus. To a *lesser degree* a father's pleasure or displeasure may be impressed upon the child especially if he has expressed a strong preference for one sex and the child turns out to be the opposite gender. Symptoms of rejection include a constant desire for physical love and assurance of self-worth.

When a baby is not bonded to its mother soon after birth, he/she may experience a sense of rejection. For the sake of survival, some babies are placed in an incubator immediately after birth. It may be days, weeks, or even months before the mother is able to show the infant motherly love. Other mothers may have insufficient milk, or refuse to breast-feed their babies, resulting in no intimate bond being established between them. Whatever the cause, the lack of tenderness and physical bonding causes feelings of rejection. Babies who are not sick and are well cared for, but who cry continuously are often expressing their need for intimacy. An adopted child, particularly, may battle with rejection.

Rejected parents often produce rejected children. Parents who have suffered from hereditary rejection, or have been rejected before marriage, many times are unable to share personal warmth with their children if they have not received deliverance. Without a doubt they do love their children, but because they have had no family example of love or feel emotionally bound, they are unable to express love physically. It is not uncommon to hear a parent say *"we are not a demonstrative family"* OR *"we aren't the kissing and hugging types,"* which probably equates to *"we are embarrassed about any demonstrations of affection."* So the children grow up feeling rejected, insecure, and lacking in self-worth despite being surrounded by material substitutes.

Often times, individuals battling with rejection respond to a question about their early childhood relationship with their parents by saying something like this: *"I know my father (or mother) loved me because they bought me things"* or *"they were kind to me."* Many feel that by confessing a feeling of rejection in childhood, they are being disloyal to their parents. And sometimes it is hurtful to be truthful, particularly if the parents are deceased. But uncovering the truth of hereditary rejection is the first step toward eradicating. All forms of rejection are roots, which need to be uprooted.

**Reflections:**

# Dynamics of Fear

Jesus expounds upon the dynamics of fear in the following parable about the talents:

**Matthew 25:14-29**

14. For it is like a man who was about to take a long journey and he called his servants together and entrusted them with his property.

15. To one he gave five talents [probably about $5,000], to another two, to another one--to each in proportion to his own personal ability. Then he departed and left the country.

16. He who had received the five talents went at once and traded with them, and he gained five talents more.

17. And likewise he who had received the two talents--he also gained two talents more.

18. But he who had received the one talent went and dug a hole in the ground and hid his master's money.

19. Now after a long time the master of those servants returned and settled accounts with them.

20. And he who had received the five talents came and brought him five more, saying, Master, you entrusted to me five talents; see, here I have gained five talents more.

21. His master said to him, Well done, you upright (honorable, admirable) and faithful servant! You have been faithful and trustworthy over a little; I will put you in charge of much. Enter into and share the joy (the delight, the blessedness) which your master enjoys.

22. And he also who had the two talents came forward, saying, Master, you entrusted two talents to me; here I have gained two talents more.

23. His master said to him, Well done, you upright (honorable, admirable) and faithful servant! You have been faithful and trustworthy over a little; I will put you in charge of much. Enter into and share the joy (the delight, the blessedness) which your master enjoys.

24. He who had received one talent also came forward, saying, Master, I knew you to be a harsh and hard man, reaping where you did not sow, and gathering where you had not winnowed [the grain].

25. So I was afraid, and I went and hid your talent in the ground. Here you have what is your own.

26. But his master answered him, you wicked and lazy and idle servant! Did you indeed know that I reap where I have not sowed and gather [grain] where I have not winnowed?

27. Then you should have invested my money with the bankers, and at my coming I would have received what was my own with interest.

28. So take the talent away from him and give it to the one who has the ten talents.

29. For to everyone who has will more be given, and he will be furnished richly so that he will have an abundance; but from the one who does not have, even what he does have will be taken away,

This is a story many can identify with: it's about three men who were each given a talent and one became immobilized by fear and feelings of inadequacy. He was so afraid of failure that he became restrained and powerless. He didn't invest the talent, nor did he use it, but buried it in the ground and tried to "play it safe." His immobilization was motivated by:

- ✓ Fear of rejection by the master,
- ✓ Fear of failure,
- ✓ Fear of comparison (to others making their investments)
- ✓ Fear of taking a risk.

This man did what so many do who are bound by fear: nothing! That's exactly why Satan continues to use this particular tactic from his old play book so often with God's people! Because it's effective: Satan knows God has gifted and placed talent in you, but if he can inflict fear on your path to destiny, you will become immobilized, just like the man above, and give-up by trying to play it safe.

This is especially true when you are wavering in the promises of God, where you start and stop what God has called you to do. You become paralyzed by the intruders of fear and give up and doubt God and His promises. Due to this, many settle into jobs, marriages, businesses, and relationships that are not the will of God, living a life far below their potential, drowning in lies, struggling with stress and depression. Giving-in to the struggles of fear and criticism will make you:

- ➡ Fearful of standing up
- ➡ Fearful of speaking the truth
- ➡ Fearful of taking a risk

Fear produces immobilization in your life and a lethargic attitude that places restraints on the dreams, visions, and prophecies God has given you.

**Reflections:**

# Anger

Anger wears many different faces and can take on many different forms:

➡ Feeling like fire

➡ Seeing red

➡ Feeling hot and sweaty

➡ Churning stomach

➡ Rising blood pressure

➡ Increasing breathing rate

➡ Boiling blood, etc.

Anger can be triggered by people and circumstances outside of you, or it can occur due to self-inflicted wounds or, from making poor choices in life. In defining your anger, examine the cause; is it:

➡ needs not being met

➡ feeling misunderstood

➡ feeling dis-respected

➡ feeling ignored

➡ not getting your way or getting your point across

➡ feeling rejected

➡ feeling fearful, or

➡ feeling your worth is not valued/devalued

External/Internal Forces

A person needs to examine whether most of his/her anger exists because of external or internal pressures. Externally, we point to someone else or to something that is the cause of our anger (blame for our pain). Internal anger can be linked to your personal worth, needs, and convictions. Compromising one's morals and values can be the foundation of one's anger; this is recklessness, where you are consistently sabotaging your emotional stability.

## Checklist

*Check the statements below that apply to you to help decide whether morality problems play a role in your anger:*

_____ I have no desire to pursue a relationship with God; I just want to attend church.

_____ I entertain lustful thoughts and fantasies more than I would like.

_____ My friends are able to persuade me to participate in activities I should avoid.

_____ I find myself cynically questioning the importance of living a holy lifestyle.

_____ At times I feel like two separate people; a good person and, privately, a conniving person.

_____ Going to church is more of a ritual for me than a truly purposeful experience.

_____ I am entertained by obscene humor or sleazy jokes.

_____ I have to struggle to maintain decency in my sexual habits.

_____ Cutting corners in my responsibilities is easier now than it was five years ago.

_____ I would rather spend a pleasure-seeking night "out on the town" than a quiet evening at home.

_____ I have had several social relationships that began with a thrill but ended in frustration.

If you checked four or more of the statements above, you can probably recall several times when anger occurred as the result of inevitable disappointment.

Godly ways to handle your anger:
- Acknowledge your anger to God – *Jeremiah 17:10*
- Pause and listen – *James 1:19*
- Repent –of your stubbornness, anger, ungodly ways – *Mark 1:15*
- Develop a relationship with the Lord – *Romans 1:11, Romans 12:2*
- Give your anger to God – *Galatians 5:22-23*
- Discipline self – *1 Corinthians 9:27*

**Reflections:**

# Self-worth

Low self-esteem is a profound feeling of inferiority, inadequacy, and low self-worth. This feeling shackles many Christians in spite of their wonderful spiritual experiences and intelligence, despite their faith and knowledge of God's word. Although they understand their position as sons and daughters of God, they are tied up in knots, bound by a terrible feeling of inferiority and chained to a deep sense of worthlessness.

Low self-esteem

New King James Version (NKJV) (1 John 4:4)

4 You are of God, little children, and have overcome them, because He who is in you is greater than he who is in the world.

New King James Version (NKJV) (Romans 8:37)

37 Yet in all these things we are more than conquerors through Him who loved us.

New King James Version (NKJV) (Galatians 3:28-29)

28 There is neither Jew nor Greek, there is neither slave nor free, there is neither male nor female; for you are all one in Christ Jesus.

29 And if you are Christ's, then you are Abraham's seed, and heirs according to the promise.

Low self-esteem is the deadliest of all of Satan's emotional and psychological weapons. There are four ways he uses this weapon to bring defeat and failure into your life:

1) **Paralyzes potential**- Very few people have fully overcome the haunting self-doubts, dragging disappointments about who they are, and what they can be. Low self-esteem begins even in the crib, continues through kindergarten, and worsens during the teen years into adult life. It seems to settle in like a great fog. Sometimes it lifts a little but always returns trying to engulf with the purpose of drowning.

2) **Destroys dreams** – "Where there is no vision, the people perish: but he that keepeth the law, happy is he," (Proverbs. 29:18 (KJV). Yes that is true. Having the wrong vision of self or having a low-esteem picture of self, being inferior and inadequate will also cause you to self-destruct. Your dreams will be destroyed and God's great plan for your life will not be fulfilled.

3) **Ruins relationships** – Satan uses your nagging sense of inferiority and inadequacy to isolate you from others, for the typical way of coping with feelings of inferiority is to pull within self and have as little contact with other people as you possibly can and just occasionally peek out as the rest of the world goes by. Who are the hardest people to get along with? Those who don't like themselves,–why? They don't like themselves, or others, and they are just hard to get along with. Low self-esteem wrecks interpersonal relationships more than anything else.

4) **Sabotages Christian service** – One can be a diligent worker in the church with a faithful weekly attendance. One can be in an intimate relationship with God, know His voice and presence, and still be deceived by Satan for the following purposes:

    →    *To stop and hinder your Christian service,*

    →    *To doubt God's calling in your life,*

    →    *To fear failure by not accomplishing what God has called you to, or*

    →    *To fear what people will say about you.*

Our self-worth is shaped and fashioned from a whole system of pictures and feelings we have nourished and taken into our minds about ourselves. Other elements that also contribute to our self-worth are un –mended and un-attended emotional wounds received from unhealthy relationships manufactured in us, which society calls "baggage."
This baggage can range from low self-esteem, bitterness, anger, inferiority, to rejection, etc.

These emotional wounds bring about internal torments or conflicts, leaving an individual with a low self-concept. Those who replay undesirable pictures over and over again in their minds can be left with a negative self-image that will eventually determine the behavior they project to others.

*There are four resources from which I believe we receive our self-concepts:*
1. Hereditary traits

2. Conception through teen years

3. Family environment

4. Relationships

# Four Resources

1. **HEREDITARY TRAITS** – Inheritance is an example of a person receiving his or her self-concept through hereditary traits. When patterns exist in families,'-a bloodline search usually exposes generational curses. This can be accomplished by research or studying the lifestyles/patterns of men and women in your family.

2. **CONCEPTION THROUGH TEEN YEARS-** I worked with an un-wed mother who carried an unwanted child to birth; her rejection of the child placed her child in jeopardy of battling with rejection and self-rejection. The spirit of rejection entered the child by traveling through the umbilical cord into the fetus. This child suffered rejection, self-rejection, shame and low self-esteem throughout her teen and young adult life. It was not until she was in her late-30' that she received deliverance through her acceptance of Christ as her Lord and Savior. Today she is a powerhouse for the Lord —well-adjusted and helping others who are battling the spirit of rejection!

3. **FAMILY ENVIRONMENT-** Family relationships can be very effective in shaping how we view and relate to one another. It's in the family that we receive our first training in how to relate in and to society. Painful pictures and hurtful memories of past experiences in the family can create stumbling blocks in life, which can prevent us from moving forward in the plans God has for our life. We become stagnated in our walk with God as we encounter very limited Christian growth. This can cause us both natural and spiritual delay concerning the things of God and movement toward our destiny. Good morals, values, respect for one another, support and encouragement must be exercised frequently within our family settings if we are to produce good sound healthy individuals both spiritually and naturally.

4. **RELATIONSHIPS** –Relationships are another source that affects how we see and/or feel about ourselves. Words are very powerful they come to life through the ears of others.

New King James Version (NKJV)
Death and life are in the power of the tongue, And those who love it will eat its fruit. (PROVERBS 18:21).

These four sources create our experiences of life right up to the present time. They tell you what you inherited from your parents, how you were treated, how you were trained, and how you relate to people. They primarily reflect your parents and family members and the messages they sent to you about yourself through their:

- facial expressions,
- vocal tones,
- attitudes,
- words, and
- actions.

Babies have little concept of self, but as they grow and gradually begin to distinguish differences, they gain a picture of themselves. How do they receive these pictures of themselves? They receive them by the reflections and reactions of the important people in their life.

## Pictures and feelings

Pictures and feelings about you arrive largely from what you see and feel reflected by your family members or love ones, as you:

- Watch their expressions,

- Hear the tone in their voices, and

- See their actions/reactions.

These reflections tell us not only who we are, but also who we can become. As the reflections gradually become part of us, we take on the shape of the person we see through the reflections of our family and our loved ones.

## *Exercise:*

Try to think of a significant person who was in your life or who is currently in your life that you respect, like, and/or admire. What message is this person sending you about yourself through his/her facial expressions, vocal tones, attitudes, words, and actions that you remember?

You may use a sheet of paper if you like, to jot down the message: think of as many messages as you can. They do not have to be all positive or negative. Once you have reviewed the messages they are sending you, review the relationship. A relationship will either make a deposit or a withdrawal in your life and hopefully it will be positive. If it's negative, review and ask yourself:

➡ Is this relationship contributing anything good to my life?

➡ Why do I feel I need to have a relationship with this person?

➡ What price am I paying to maintain this relationship in my life?

➡ Is it worth it?

**Reflections:**

www.ingramcontent.com/pod-product-compliance
Lightning Source LLC
Chambersburg PA
CBHW080054280326
41934CB00014B/3310